IT'S TIME TO EAT RHUBARB

It's Time to Eat RHUBARB

Walter the Educator

Silent King Books
A WhichHead Entertainment Imprint

Copyright © 2025 by Walter the Educator

All rights reserved. No part of this book may be reproduced in any manner whatsoever without written per- mission except in the case of brief quotations embodied in critical articles and reviews.

First Printing, 2024

Disclaimer

This book is a literary work; the story is not about specific persons, locations, situations, and/or circumstances unless mentioned in a historical context. Any resemblance to real persons, locations, situations, and/or circumstances is coincidental. This book is for entertainment and informational purposes only. The author and publisher offer this information without warranties expressed or implied. No matter the grounds, neither the author nor the publisher will be accountable for any losses, injuries, or other damages caused by the reader's use of this book. The use of this book acknowledges an understanding and acceptance of this disclaimer.

It's Time to Eat RHUBARB is a collectible early learning book by Walter the Educator suitable for all ages belonging to Walter the Educator's Time to Eat Book Series. Collect more books at WaltertheEducator.com

USE THE EXTRA SPACE TO TAKE NOTES AND DOCUMENT YOUR MEMORIES

RHUBARB

It's time to eat, hooray, hooray!

It's Time to Eat
Rhubarb

A special treat is on its way.

It's red and green and tart but sweet,

A tasty snack that can't be beat!

This funny plant has stalks so tall,

But don't eat leaves, no, not at all!

The stems are yummy, bright, and red,

In pies and jams or warm with bread!

Take a bite, it's sour, wow!

But sugar makes it sweet somehow.

Cook it soft or eat it raw,

Crunchy, juicy, best of all!

Grandma makes her famous treat,

A rhubarb pie that's hard to beat!

She adds some berries, red and bright,

And bakes it golden, what a sight!

It's Time to Eat
Rhubarb

Brother stirs the rhubarb jam,

Spreading sweetness, yes, he can!

On toast, on biscuits, warm and light,

It makes each morning feel so bright!

Mom says, "Rhubarb's good for you,

With vitamins and fiber too!"

It helps our tummies feel just right,

And keeps us strong with every bite!

Dad likes rhubarb in a stew,

Mixed with apples, what a view!

A little sour, a little sweet,

It makes our dinner quite a treat!

Sister takes a tiny taste,

She says, "Oh wow, I love this paste!"

"It's pink and yummy, tart and fun,

It's Time to Eat
Rhubarb

I think I'll have another one!"

So when it's time to eat again,

Try rhubarb with your food, my friend!

A pie, a jam, a tasty bite,

It makes each meal feel just right!

Now our plates are nice and clean,

Rhubarb made our bellies gleam!

Thank you, rhubarb, pink and bright,

It's Time to Eat
Rhubarb

For bringing us such pure delight!

ABOUT THE CREATOR

Walter the Educator is one of the pseudonyms for Walter Anderson. Formally educated in Chemistry, Business, and Education, he is an educator, an author, a diverse entrepreneur, and he is the son of a disabled war veteran. "Walter the Educator" shares his time between educating and creating. He holds interests and owns several creative projects that entertain, enlighten, enhance, and educate, hoping to inspire and motivate you. Follow, find new works, and stay up to date with Walter the Educator™

at WaltertheEducator.com

www.ingramcontent.com/pod-product-compliance
Lightning Source LLC
LaVergne TN
LVHW052014060526
838201LV00059B/4033